# Paleo BBQ

*Quick, Easy and Delicious Recipes*

# Disclaimer

## Summary

Many people consider paleo to be a very restricted diet where they cannot enjoy different tastes or ingredients. Well, people cannot be more wrong because you can enjoy almost anything in paleo all you have to do is stay away from processed foods and some other food items that are not going to do you any good and you are all set to go. Since summers are just round the corner we decided to give your taste buds a tasty treat and therefore we combined for you delicious paleo BBQ recipes that you can prepare in your backyard while enjoying the hot summer breeze.

In this recipe book you will find:

1.  Delectable Paleo BBQ recipes that you can cook in backyard parties or picnics.

2.  Nutritional information for each recipe to help you keep track of your calories.

3.  Serving size to help you plan your meals beforehand.

4.  Cooking time so that you can plan your day accordingly.

5.  Recipes of paleo friendly sauces and condiments that you can prepare at home.

We have included easy-to-cook recipes that you can enjoy in this summer season with your loved ones. So tie your apron and get the grill ready in your backyard to enjoy these mouthwatering recipes.

# Contents

# Introduction

Paleo is the diet that our ancestors used to follow. It is a diet that is free from all kinds of chemically processed foods and allows you to eat all that is natural and real. It is also known as cavemen diet and it is all about eating what our ancestors used to eat.

Some 12,000 years ago our ancestors used to live, longer, and healthier lives and one of the major causes of this was the diet that they used to live on. Our ancestors consumed what they could hunt along with fruits, vegetables, plants, nuts, and seeds that were available to them naturally.

Due to the ever increasing diseases that we are exposed to these days, scientists were forced to find out ways in which the quality of our lives can be improved. Hence researches were done and studies were conducted on Paleo lifestyle and the results were astonishingly positive. People how followed this diet experienced the following symptoms:

1. Significant increase in their energy levels
2. Normal blood pressure
3. A drop in cholesterol levels
4. Decline in body fat
5. Normal blood sugar levels

These are just a few of the many benefits that majority of the people following this diet experience. This is the reason why we have compiled for you delicious BBQ Paleo recipes that you can cook and enjoy this summer season.

So get, set, ready, to delve into the delicious BBQ recipes that are easy to cook and good to eat.

# Paleo BBQ Homemade Sauces

## Paleo Ketchup

**Yields** 1.5 cups

**Cooking time** One Night

**Nutritional Information:** Calories 17, Total Fat 0g, Protein 0.5g, Carbohydrates 3.7g

*A simple recipe that will help you prepare paleo friendly ketchup at home*

**Ingredients**

Cayenne pepper – 1/8 teaspoon

Allspice (ground) – 1 pinch

Garlic cloves – 1 pinch

Salt – ¼ teaspoon

Cinnamon – ¼ teaspoon

Water – 1/3 cup

Mustard (dry) – ¼ teaspoon

Lemon juice – 2 tablespoon

Tomato paste – 6 ounces

## Directions to Prepare

1. Take a medium sized bowl and combine all the ingredients in it with the help of a whip.
2. Place the mixture in the refrigerator for a night and allow the flavors to enhance overnight.
3. Enjoy homemade ketchup with all your meals.

# Worcestershire Sauce

**Yields** 2 cups

**Cooking time** 15 minutes

**Nutritional Information per 100 grams:** Calories 78, Total Fat 0g, Protein 0.5g,

Carbohydrates 19g

*Prepare the delicious Worcestershire sauce in your home with this simple recipe*

**Ingredients**

Fresh black pepper (ground) – 1/8 teaspoon

Cinnamon – 1/8 teaspoon

Garlic powder – ¼ teaspoon

Onion powder – ¼ teaspoon

Mustard powder – ¼ teaspoon

Ginger (ground) – ¼ teaspoon

Water – 2 tablespoon

Lemon juice – ½ cup

## Directions to Prepare

1. Take a sauce pan and combine all the ingredients in it.

2. Place the pan on stove and bring the ingredients to boil with frequent stirring.

3. Allow the ingredients to simmer for around a minute until all the ingredients are well incorporated and allow the flavors to enhance and develop.

4. Allow the mixture to cool and then store in the refrigerator.

5. Enjoy your homemade, chemical-free Worcestershire sauce.

# Paleo Homemade Mustard

**Yields** 1 cup

**Cooking time** 15 minutes

**Nutritional Information per 100 grams:** Calories 9, Total Fat 0.2g, Protein 0.2g, Carbohydrates 0.3g

*Homemade mustard that is easy to prepare and as good as any you will find in the grocery stores*

**Ingredients**

Sea salt – to taste

Water – ½ cup

Mustard powder – ½ cup

## Directions to Prepare

1. Take a bowl and add water and mustard powder in it and combine well.

2. To add more seasoning you can add lemon zest or lemon or freshly chopped basil or parsley to give it a taste that you prefer.

3. Allow the mixture to stand for at least 15 minutes (and more if you have time) and enjoy the fresh flavors.

.

# BBQ Sauce

**Yields** 2 cup

**Cooking time** 45 minutes

**Nutritional Information:** Calories 172, Total Fat 0.6g, Protein 0.8g, Carbohydrates 41g

*Homemade BBQ sauce that is easy to prepare and with a nice smoky touch to it*

**Ingredients**

Paprika (smoked)

Cinnamon – 1 pinch

Garlic cloves (ground) – 1 pinch

Worcestershire sauce (homemade) – 1 tablespoon

Mustard (homemade) – 3 tablespoon

Ketchup (homemade) – ¼ cup

Water – ½ cup

Apple cider vinegar - ½ cup

Tomato paste - 6 ounces

Minced garlic clove – 1

Minced onion – 1

**Direction to Prepare**

1. Add a little cooking fat in a drying pan and add onions in it.

2. Allow the onions to brown for about 4 minutes.

3. Add garlic in the pan and cook for one more minute.

4. Place all the other ingredients in the pan and allow the contents of the pan to simmer for about half an hour.

5. After half an hour, taste the sauce and adjust the flavor by adding more vinegar or smoked paprika if you desire.

6. Allow the sauce to cool and place it in the refrigerator.

7. Enjoy as a sauce or a side condiment with chicken or beef.

# Ghee

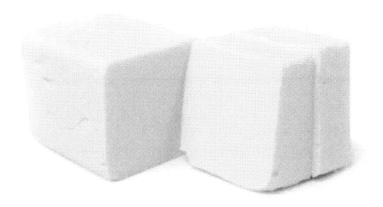

**Yields** 2 cup

**Cooking time** 45 minutes

**Nutritional Information per 56 grams:** Calories 407, Total Fat 46g, Protein 0g,

Carbohydrates 0g

*Homemade BBQ sauce that is easy to prepare and with a nice smoky touch to it*

**Ingredients**

Glass jar

Paper towel or cheese cloth

Mesh strainer

Slotted spoon

A large stainless or wooden spoon

Pot with heavy bottom

Butter – 1 pound

## Directions for Preparations

1. Place the heavy bottomed pot on low heat and add butter in it to slowly melt the butter.

2. Make sure that you do not stir the butter at all while it is melting in the pot but keep the temperature very low.

3. Once all the butter is melted, use a slotted spoon to remove the froth from top.

4. Use paper towel or cheese cloth to line the mesh strainer and place it over a bowl or a jar and pour the melted butter over it.

5. Once in the bowl, allow the butter to stand for a minute, allowing the fat and water to separate.

6. Finally remove the butter and transfer it to a glass jar. Make sure that no water from the bottom of the bowl gets mixed with the butter in the glass jar.

7. Use this ghee for all the paleo cooking.

# Paleo Applesauce

**Serves** 4

**Cooking time** 45 minutes

**Nutritional Information:** Calories 68, Total Fat 0.2g, Protein 0.2g, Carbohydrates 17g

*An amazingly simple and delicious applesauce recipe that will make your mouth*

*water*

**Ingredients**

Sea salt – to taste

Fresh nutmeg (ground) – 1 pinch

Cinnamon (ground) – ½ teaspoon

Ghee – 2 tablespoon

Lemon juice (fresh) – 1 teaspoon

Honey (raw) – 6 tablespoon

Water – ¼ cup

Apples (sliced and peeled) – 3pound

**Directions to Prepare**

1. Heat the oven to 425 degrees Fahrenheit.

2. In a baking dish mix salt, ghee, lemon juice, honey, water and apples.

3. Place the baking dish in the pre-heated oven and roast for about 30 minutes or until they turn very tender and soft.

4. Transfer the content of the baking dish in a bowl and puree the apple with the help of a food mill or a hand mixer.

5. Add in all the spices to the puree and mix until all the ingredients are well combined.

6. You can serve it hot or cold according to your desire.

# Paleo BBQ Recipes

## Grilled Marinated Flank Steak

**Serves** 4

**Prep time** 8 hours

**Cooking Time** 30 minutes

**Nutritional Information:** Calories 165, Total Fat 7.1g, Protein 23.6g, Carbohydrates 15g

*Tender steaks with well incorporated flavors that you can enjoy with your family and friends in a BBQ picnic*

**Ingredients**

Chili powder – 1 tsp

Thyme (dried) – 2 tsp

Salt – 1 tbsp

Onion (dried and chopped) – 1 tbsp

Paprika – 1 tbsp

Fresh ginger (grated) – 1 tbsp

Crushed garlic – 6 cloves

Mustard – 2 tbsp

Lime juice – 1 lemon

Vinegar (apple cider) – ½ cup

Coconut aminos – 2/3 cup

Coconut oil – 1 cup

Flank steak – 3 pounds

## Directions for Preparation

1. Slice the flank into pieces that you can easily manage.

2. Combine all the ingredients (except steak) to prepare marinade and mix well until all the ingredients are well incorporated.

3. Place each piece of steak in a Ziploc bag and equally divide the prepared marinade in each bag.

4. Seal the bags and allow the steaks to marinade overnight.

5. Now all you have to do is to simply grill the marinated steaks and enjoy!

# Paleo Chicken Wings

**Serves** 4

**Prep time** 1 to 3 hours

**Cooking time** 30 minutes

**Nutritional Information per chicken wing:** Calories 81, Total Fat 5.4g, Protein 7.46g, Carbohydrates 0g

*Juicy chicken wings that you can enjoy as a snack with or a starter*

**Ingredients**

BBQ sauce (homemade) – 1 cup

BBQ rub

Chicken wings – 24

**Ingredients for BBQ Rub**

Sea salt – to taste

Black pepper – to taste

Minced rosemary – 1 teaspoon

Onion powder – 1 teaspoon

Cumin – 1 teaspoon

Garlic powder – 1 teaspoon

Chili powder – 2 teaspoon

Paprika – 2 tablespoon

**Directions for Preparations**

1. Combine all the ingredients for the BBQ rub in a small bowl and mix until all the ingredients are well combined.

2. Use black pepper and salt to season to taste.

3. Coat the chicken wing with BBQ rub and place them in a freezer bag and refrigerate for at least 2 hours or overnight.

4. Prepare the homemade BBQ sauce by following the recipe given earlier in the book.

5. Transfer the marinated wings into a big bowl and mix 1 cup of BBQ sauce in them.

6. Heat the oven to 350 degree Fahrenheit.

7. Place the sauce coated and marinated wings in a baking sheet and place the sheet in the pre heated oven and bake for about 20 minutes. Make sure that you turn them at least once after 10 minutes.

8. After baking the wings for about 20 minutes turn the oven to high broil and roast chicken wings from both sides for 5 minutes each.

9. Serve hot, right out of the oven, with extra BBQ sauce for dipping.

## BBQ Chicken with Blueberry Maple

**Serves** 4

**Cooking time** 45 minutes

**Nutritional Information per 100 grams:** Calories 400, Total Fat 16g, Protein 32g, Carbohydrates 32g

*Juice chicken tender that you can enjoy with a nice cold beverage on a nice summer day*

**Ingredients**

Black pepper – 1 tsp

Sea salt - 1 tsp

Garlic (minced) – 2 tbsp

BBQ rub (same ingredients that were used in Paleo Chicken wings recipe) – 3 tbsp

Chicken tenders – 2 pounds

BBQ sauce (Homemade)

## Directions for Preparation

1. Prepare BBQ sauce by following the same instructions given earlier in the book.

2. While your sauce is being prepared, marinade the chicken pieces.

3. Take a large bowl and combine all the ingredients of chicken season in it.

4. Generously coat the chicken pieces in the mix.

5. Transfer the BBQ sauce to a small bowl and use a brush to coat the chicken pieces with the sauce.

6. Place the chicken pieces on the prepared grill and brush some more sauce on the top.

7. Flip the chicken as it starts to whiten and gets puffed up.

8. Make sure that the chicken is properly cooked from both sides. Remove the pieces from the grill and allow it to sit for about 5 minutes.

9. Coat the grilled pieces with the BBQ sauce generously.

10. Serve hot and enjoy.

# Chicken Kebabs

**Serves** 6

**Cooking time** 1 hour and 30 minutes

**Nutritional Information:** Calories 270, Total Fat 6g, Protein 47g, Carbohydrates 6.5g

*Juice chicken tender cooked on skewers.*

**Ingredients**

Black pepper (ground) – to taste

Chicken breast (free-range organic) – 2 pounds (chopped into 1 ½ inch pieces)

Skewers (bamboo)

Minced garlic – 2 cloves

Grated ginger (fresh) – 2 tsp

White vinegar – 1 tsp

Honey (raw organic) – 1 tbsp

Water – ¼ cup

White wine – ¼ cup

Soy-sauce (organic wheat free) – ¼ cup

**Directions for Preparation**

1. Place a small sauce on medium flames and add garlic, ginger, white vinegar, honey, water, white wine and soy sauce in it.

2. Bring the mixture to boil and then lower the flowers. Allow to mixture to dimmer on low heat for about 5 minutes.

3. Turn the heat off and allow the mixture to cool for at least 10 minutes.

4. Take a Ziploc bag or sealable container and combine the mixture with the chicken pieces. Cover the container or seal the bag and keep in the refrigerator to marinate for about 30 minutes.

5. Soak bamboo stick in water for about 5 minutes.

6. Remove the chicken pieces from the bag and skewer them on the soaked bamboo sticks.

7. Heat a grill pan or a grill to medium-low.

8. Low temperature is recommended to glaze the teriyaki marinade without burning it black.

9. Grill the chucks of chicken until they are golden brown and completely cooked through, for about 10 to 12 minutes by regularly turning them.

10. When the juices run clear, transfer the chunks to a serving plate.

11. Garnish with chopped cilantro.

12. Serve hot.

# Chicken Burgers with Sweet Potato Crispy Fries

**Serves** 4

**Cooking time** 1 hour

**Nutritional Information per 100 grams:** Calories 490, Total Fat 8g, Protein 63g, Carbohydrates 63g

*Delicious and juice chicken burgers served with crispy sweet potatoes fries and homemade Paleo BBQ sauce*

## Ingredients

Sea salt

Avocado oil – 2 to 3 tbsp

Sweet potatoes – 1 to 2

Olive oil (for cooking) – 1 tbsp

BBQ sauce – for garnish

Sliced onion – 1

Sea salt – ¼ tsp

Black pepper – ¼ tsp

Garlic powder – 1 tsp

Onion powder – 1 tsp

Smoked paprika – 1 tsp

Ground chicken (organic free range) – 1 to 1.5 pounds

**Directions for Preparing Chicken Burgers**

1. Take a bowl and add ground chicken in it.

2. Add pepper, salt, spices, and BBQ sauce in the chicken and mix well.

3. Take a large skillet and place it on medium high-high heat and add olive oil in it.

4. Use your hands to form burgers from the chicken mixture.

5. Make 4 to 5 patties and then place them in a hot skillet.

6. Cook for about 8 minutes from each side or until they are properly cooked through.

7. While the burgers are cooking, take a small skillet and add a little olive oil in it.

8. Add sliced onion in the skillet with a little salt and caramelize them a little for about 10 minutes.

**Directions for Preparing Sweet Potato Fries**

1. Heat the oven to 400 degrees.

2. Slice the sweet potatoes with their skin still on.

3. Slice them to your desired thickness but remember the thinner the crispier.

4. Transfer the sliced potatoes in a large bowl and add salt and avocado oil in it.

5. Stir them around until all the slices are nicely coated with oil and salt.

6. Take a cooking sheet and line it with parchment paper.

7. Place the fries on the prepared cookie sheet.

8. Spread out the fries so that they are not overlapping. You might have to use two sheets depending on the thickness of the fries.

9. Place the sheet in the preheated oven and cook for about 25 to 30 minutes or until the fries reach the desired crispiness.

**Directions for Serving**

1. Once the burgers are properly cooked through, place them on a serving plate and garnish with BBQ sauce.

2. Place some crispy fries on the side and serve hot.

3. You are good to go!

# BBQ Ribs with Applesauce

**Serves** 4

**Prep time** 25 minutes + 12 hours

**Cooking Time** 3 hours and 30 minutes

**Nutritional Information per 100 grams:** Calories 330, Total Fat 21g, Protein 18g, Carbohydrates 18g

*Mouthwatering ribs soaked in BBQ applesauce making it simply irresistible.*

**Ingredients**

Beef ribs (organic free-range) – 5 to 6 pounds

**Ingredients for BBQ Rub**

Black pepper (freshly ground) – to taste

Sea salt

Minced garlic - 4 cloves

Mustard (ground) – 2 teaspoon

Oregano (dried) – 1 tablespoon

Paprika – 2 tablespoon

Chili powder – 2 tablespoon

**Ingredients for BBQ Applesauce**

Black pepper (freshly ground) – to taste

Sea salt – to taste

Paprika – 1 tablespoon

Chili powder – 2 tablespoon

Vinegar (apple cider) – 3 tablespoon

Clarified butter – 3 tablespoon

Minced garlic – 3 cloves

Minced onion -1/2

Applesauce (homemade) – 1 cup

Ketchup (homemade) – 1 ½ cup

**Directions for Preparations**

1. Combine all the ingredients of BBQ run in a small bowl.

2. Run the mixture on both sides of the ribs and place them in the refrigerator for about 8 to 12 hours so that the flavors get well incorporated.

3. Heat the oven to 250 degree Fahrenheit.

4. Place the marinated ribs on a baking sheet and bake in the preheated oven for about 1 ½ hours.

5. While the ribs are cooking start preparing the BBQ applesauce.

6. Take a saucepan and place clarified butter in it.

7. Add garlic and onions in the saucepan and cook until they are tender and soft.

8. The add pepper, salt, paprika, cinnamon, chili powder, applesauce, ketchup, and apple cider vinegar in it.

9. Let the content of the saucepan simmer for about 30 minutes.

10. Baste the ribs with the prepared sauce and continue cooking for another 30 minutes, basting on each side with the sauce after every 10 minutes.

11. Take the ribs out of the oven once they are properly cooked through.

12. Heat the grill or broiler.

13. Grill or broil the ribs for about 5 minutes from each side and serve hot.

14. To add more taste you can broil the ribs before grilling.

# Shredded BBQ Paleo Chicken

**Serves** 4

**Cooking time** 1 hour

**Nutritional Information per 100 grams:** Calories 180, Total Fat 6g, Protein 8g, Carbohydrates 2g

*Delicious and juice chicken shreds combined with the savory sauce*

## Ingredients

Paleo hot sauce – 1 tsp

Black pepper – 1 tsp

Sea salt – 1 tsp

Honey (organic) – 3 tbsp

Tomato paste – 2 tbsp

Crushed tomatoes – ½ cup

Apple cider vinegar – 1 ½ cup

Crushed garlic – 3 cloves

Minced onion – ½ white

Paleo homemade ghee – 2 tbsp

Whole chicken – 1 (whole)

**Directions for Preparations**

1. Thoroughly rinse the chicken and pat dry it.

2. Place the prepared chicken in a slow cooker and season with pepper and salt.

3. Cook on high heat settings for about 3 hours.

4. In the meantime, take a large sauce pan and melt ghee in it.

5. Add minced onions in the pan and cook until soft for about 4 to 5 minutes.

6. Add hot sauce, black pepper, sea salt, honey, tomato paste, crushed tomatoes, vinegar, and garlic in the pan and stir until the mixture boils.

7. Reduce the heat to low and allow the mixture to simmer.

8. Reduce the sauce until it remains quarter to a third. It should be thick but not in the form of a paste.

9. Remove the chicken from slow cooker and shred all the meat.

10. Combine it with the savory sauce and serve.

# Steak Skewers Garnished With Cherry BBQ Sauce

**Serves** 4

**Cooking time** 1 hour

**Nutritional Information per 100 grams:** Calories 490, Total Fat 8g, Protein 63g,

Carbohydrates 63g

*Mouth waters steaks on skewers soaked in cherry BBQ Sauce*

**Ingredients for the Cherry BBQ Sauce**

Pepper (freshly ground) – to taste

Sea salt – to taste

Chopped cherries (frozen) – 10 ounces

Apple juice – ¼ cup

Balsamic vinegar – ¼ cup

Coconut aminos – ¼ cup

Tomato paste – 1 tbsp

Peeled ginger (grated) – 1 inch

Minced garlic – 1 clove

Minced shallot – ½ cup

Ghee – 2 tsp

**Ingredients for Steak Skewers**

Finely sliced scallions – ¼ cup

Ghee (melted) – 2 tbsp

Ground pepper – to taste

Sea salt – to taste

Flack steak – 1 ½ pounds

**Directions for Preparations**

1. Take a small sauce pan and melt ghee in it.

2. Add shallots in the pan and season it with sauce to taste. Sauté for about 5 minutes until translucent.

3. Add tomato paste, garlic, and ginger in the pan.

4. Cook for about 30 seconds or until the mixture is fragrant.

5. Add juice vinegar, and coconut aminos and cherries and bring the mixture to a boil.

6. Reduce the heat and allow the mixture to simmer until the cherries are thickened for about 10 minutes.

7. While the mixture is cooking, occasionally stir and smash the cherries.

8. Use pepper and salt to season the sauce.

9. Pour the sauce in a bowl and keep it aside.

10. Soak 16 bamboo sticks half an hour before you want to start grilling your steak.

11. Cut the flack steak into 16 pieces.

12. First slice in half length wise, then in half across, and then in fourths, and then in eights.

13. Carefully place each slice of meat in the soaked skewer.

14. Once you have placed all the pieces in skewers, take a meat pounder and smack each steak until it is 1.2 inch in thickness.

15. Use pepper and salt to season the steaks.

16. Use ghee to brush both the sides of the steak.

17. Prepare the grill and cook for about 1 to 2 minutes from each side on high heat.

18. Allow the skewers to cool for about 5 to 10 minutes before garnishing with berry BBQ sauce.

19. Garnish with green scallion if you like and serve hot.

# Paleo BBQ Wings

**Serves** 4

**Prep time** 1 to 3 hours

**Cooking time** 30 minutes

**Nutritional Information:** Calories 61, Total Fat 4.2g, Protein 5g, Carbohydrates0.5g

*Sizzling chicken wings served with BBQ sauce*

**Ingredients**

BBQ sauce – 1 cup

BBQ rub

Chicken wings – 4 pounds (about 24)

## Ingredients for BBQ Rub

Black pepper – to taste

Sea salt – to taste

Minced rosemary – 1 teaspoon

Cumin – 1 teaspoon

Onion powder – 1 teaspoon

Garlic powder – 1 teaspoon

Chili powder – 2 teaspoon

Paprika – 2 tablespoon

**Ingredients for BBQ Sauce**

Black pepper – to taste

Sea salt - to taste

Honey (raw) – 1/3 cup

Cayenne pepper – 1 teaspoon

Chili powder – 2 teaspoon

Worcestershire sauce (homemade) – 1/3 cup

White wine – ¼ cup

Ghee – 3 tablespoon

Minced garlic – 3 cloves

Minced onion (white) – ½

Ketchup (homemade) – 2 cups

**Directions for Preparations**

1. Combine all the ingredients for the rub in a small bowl and season to taste with pepper and salt.

2. Coat the chicken wings in the rub and place them in a bag.

3. Refrigerate for 2 to 12 hours.

4. Heat the oven to 350 degrees.

5. For the BBQ sauce, heat ghee in saucepan and add onion and garlic in it.

6. Cook until they are tender and soft.

7. Add the rest of the sauce ingredients in the pan and mix until all the ingredients are well incorporated.

8. Season the sauce to your taste.

9. Allow the sauce to simmer for about half an hour.

10. Transfer wings to a bowl and add 1 cup BBQ sauce in them.

11. Mix well until all the wings are properly coated with the sauce.

12. Place the wings on a baking sheet and cook for about 20 minutes in the preheated oven.

13. Turn the wings once after 10 minutes.

14. After 20 minutes are over, turn the oven to a high broil and allow the wings to roast for about 5 minutes from each side.

15. Remove wings from oven and serve hot with BBQ sauce as a side dipping sauce.

## BBQ Paleo Meatballs

**Serves** 4

**Prep time** 15 minutes

**Cooking time** 45 minutes

**Nutritional Information:** Calories 170, Total Fat 12g, Protein 15g, Carbohydrates 6g

*Delicious and juicy meatballs served with homemade paleo BBQ sauce*

## Ingredients

Sea salt – to taste

Black pepper (ground) – to taste

Ghee

Chili powder – ½ teaspoon

Egg – 1

Almond flour – ¼ cup

Thinly sliced green onions – ½ cup

Ground beef – 2 pounds

**Directions for Preparations**

1. Heat the oven to 350 degrees Fahrenheit.

2. Mix pepper, salt, chili powder, almond flour, egg, onion, and ground beef in a bowl and combine until all the ingredients are well incorporated.

3. Roll the mixture of beef and form bit size balls and keep them aside.

4. Place a skillet over medium heat and heat ghee in it and transfer the prepared meatballs in the skillet and cook for about 4 to 5 minutes until brown from all sides.

5. Place the meatballs in a baking dish.

6. Make BBA sauce following the same instructions as mentioned in the earlier recipes.

7. Bake meatballs in the preheated oven for about 40 to 50 minutes.

8. Pour BBQ sauce over them and serve.

## Conclusion

Summers are here and so is the picnic season. Be it in your own backyard, a park or a beach, enjoying delicious BBQ with your loved never gets old. And now you can do it Paleo style!

You no longer have to waste your time searching the aisles for the Paleo sauces as you can now prepare them right in your home.

So get your grill ready and tie your apron. Start trying these recipes today and enjoy a delicious meal with your loved ones right in your backyard.

Printed in Great Britain
by Amazon